Quick and Simple Cooking for Two

From the smiles of pleasure and enjoyment with the results, everyone will think you've spent hours and hours in the preparation of these recipes . . . which make cooking for two so very easy . . .

And we've included a section on special dinners for entertaining; appetizers to very special desserts to serve as many as ten.

It's the ideal cookbook for those who don't have a lot of time to spend in the kitchen but want truly delicious meals.

We've included suggestions on how to shop for two . . . how to measure foods in quantities for two . . . storage tips on freezing, storing, and preserving main dishes for those most convenient 'planned overs' . . . food hints, food fashions, and uses for dried herbs . . .

And sprinkled throughout these recipes for soups and sandwiches—salads and main dishes—vegetables, casseroles and desserts—are bits and pieces of poetry and a touch of photography and art . . .

. . . to make your cooking for two (or more) quick, simple, and delicious!

CONTENTS

Corned Beef Waffle Grill

CORNED BEEF WAFFLE GRILL

4 slices white or whole wheat bread
4 slices American cheese
  Sliced corned beef
  Soft butter

For each sandwich, cover bottom slice of bread with cheese slice, corned beef and second slice of cheese and bread. Spread outside of sandwich with butter; grill in hot waffle iron until golden brown.

BROILED OPEN-FACE HAMBURGER SANDWICHES

½ lb. ground chuck
 4 hamburger rolls, cut in half
  Salt
  Pepper

Divide ground chuck into 8 equal parts. Place hamburger rolls cut side up on baking sheet. Spread each with hamburger meat. Season with salt and pepper. Place under broiler and cook until brown.

Beef Steak Sandwiches Mediterranean

BEEF STEAK SANDWICHES MEDITERRANEAN

1 8-oz. can tomato sauce
½ c. grated parmesan cheese
2 t. instant minced onion
1 t. oregano
  Dash garlic powder
2 large English muffins
4 beef cubed steaks
2 T. lard or drippings
4 slices mozzarella cheese
½ t. oregano
½ t. basil
4 large stuffed green olives, sliced

Combine tomato sauce, parmesan cheese, onion, oregano and garlic powder. Simmer 5 minutes. Split and toast English muffins. Brown cubed steaks, on both sides, in lard over moderate heat 7 to 10 minutes. Place each browned steak on English muffin half. Spread 2 tablespoons tomato mixture on each steak. Cover each with a slice of mozzarella cheese. Mix ½ teaspoon oregano and basil and sprinkle a little on each slice. Arrange slices of stuffed green olives on tops. Place under broiler 3 inches from heat until cheese melts, about 5 minutes. Serve 2, freeze 2.

FRENCH TOASTED CHEESE SANDWICHES

4 slices American cheese
4 slices white bread
1 egg
1½ T. milk
2 T. butter

For each sandwich, cover bottom slice of bread with 2 cheese slices and second slice of bread. Press firmly together. Beat egg and milk together in a shallow dish. Add sandwiches, one at a time to the mixture, coating each side. Sauté in butter, until golden brown on both sides.

EASTERN SANDWICH

2 t. butter
2 eggs
2 T. water
¼ c. minced ham
2 toasted buns

Beat eggs with water until blended; add ham. Melt butter in a small frying pan. Add ham mixture and cook until golden brown on both sides. Serve on toasted bun.

REUBEN SANDWICH

4 slices rye bread
1 T. mustard
2 T. sauerkraut
4 slices corned beef
4 slices Swiss cheese
1 T. butter

On each of 2 slices of bread, spread ½ tablespoon mustard; top with 1 tablespoon sauerkraut. Arrange 2 slices of corned beef and 2 slices of Swiss cheese on each; top with remaining slices of bread. Butter outside of each sandwich, using ½ T. of butter; grill until cheese begins to melt.

Variation: substitute dairy sour cream flavored to taste with chili sauce and prepared horseradish sauce for the mustard.

CHEESE STRATA

8 slices day-old white bread
6 slices American cheese
2 T. parmesan cheese
¼ t. salt
¼ t. pepper
3 eggs
1 c. milk
½ c. cream of mushroom soup
¼ c. mushrooms
Butter

Remove crusts from bread and butter one side of each slice. Place 4 of these butter side down, in a 9 x 9-inch pan. Cover evenly with the American cheese slices, then sprinkle with parmesan cheese, salt and pepper. Place remaining slices of bread on top, butter side up. Beat eggs and milk together and pour over bread. Refrigerate for several hours or overnight. When ready to bake, set pan in larger pan which has been filled with water to a depth of ½ inch. Bake at 325° for 45 minutes. While it is baking, combine mushroom soup and can of mushrooms, using only mushroom liquid to dilute the soup. Heat and serve over strata.

Mrs. P. G. Dennison

 SALADS

CRABMEAT SALAD

1 6½-oz. can crabmeat
¼ c. celery, chopped
  Dash salt
½ t. lemon juice
2 T. mayonnaise

Place all ingredients in a small bowl; toss well. Refrigerate until ready to serve.

CARROT SALAD

1 c. shredded carrots
  Few sprigs parsley
1 T. green pepper, chopped
3 T. French dressing
  Lettuce

Mix together carrots, parsley and green pepper. Toss with dressing. Serve on lettuce.

FRUIT SALAD

1 8½-oz. can pineapple
  Lettuce leaves
1 c. cottage cheese
6 whole strawberries
1 orange, peeled and sliced
¼ c. mayonnaise

Arrange lettuce leaves on 2 separate plates; place a scoop of cottage cheese on each. Drain pineapple, reserving 2 tablespoons liquid. Arrange fruit on each plate. Combine mayonnaise with reserved pineapple juice; serve with salad.

WALDORF SALAD

1 small pear, diced
1 small eating apple, diced
1 stalk celery, diced
2 T. chopped pecans
¼ c. salad dressing
1 T. orange juice
2 lettuce leaves

Mix together pear, apple, celery and nuts. Blend salad dressing and orange juice. Add to salad mixture; toss to mix. Serve on lettuce.

HOT CHICKEN SALAD

½ c. chicken, cut up
1 c. cream of chicken soup
1 T. minced onion
¼ c. toasted almonds (optional)
¼ t. salt
1 hard-boiled egg
6 T. mayonnaise
½ c. diced celery
1 T. lemon juice
½ c. potato chips

Mix all ingredients together except potato chips. Pour into a casserole and sprinkle with potato chips. Bake in a preheated 375° oven 30 minutes.

TOSSED SALAD

¼ small head lettuce
1 tomato
1 small cucumber, sliced
1 small green onion, thinly sliced
2 T. vegetable oil
1 T. wine vinegar
⅛ t. salt
⅛ t. pepper
½ clove garlic, pressed
  Dash Worcestershire sauce
1 t. crushed oregano

Break lettuce into salad bowl. Add tomato cut in eighths, cucumber and onion. Combine oil, vinegar, salt, pepper, garlic, Worcestershire sauce and oregano in a small jar with tightly fitting lid. Shake well. Toss dressing with vegetables, using two forks.

Pictured opposit
Waldorf Salad

CHEF SALAD

½ head lettuce
1 c. spinach leaves
1 c. cooked ham, slivered
½ c. cooked turkey, slivered
¼ lb. Swiss cheese, slivered
4 radishes, sliced
½ cucumber, thinly sliced
6 cherry tomatoes
½ c. croutons

Wash lettuce leaves; chill until ready to use. Line salad bowl with lettuce leaves. Break remaining lettuce into bite-size pieces and place in bowl. Add remaining ingredients, tossing to mix. Serve with salad dressing of your choice.

COLESLAW

1½ c. crisp shredded cabbage
¼ c. green pepper, chopped
1 small carrot, grated
1½ T. vinegar
1 T. water
1 T. vegetable oil
1½ T. sugar
½ t. celery seed
½ t. salt
Dash pepper

Mix together cabbage, green pepper and carrot. Combine remaining ingredients; pour over cabbage.

TOMATO SALAD

2 tomatoes, peeled
½ t. salt
½ small onion, minced
½ t. lemon juice
1 hard-boiled egg, sliced
Lettuce leaves
Dash parmesan cheese

Core tomatoes, scoop out the centers and mince. Combine salt, onion, lemon juice and egg and add to tomatoes. Arrange on lettuce leaves, and top with parmesan cheese.

TOSSED GREEN SALAD

½ small head lettuce
1 medium tomato, quartered
½ cucumber, thinly sliced
3 radishes, sliced

Wash lettuce leaves and set aside to dry. Tear lettuce into bite-size pieces and place in salad bowl. Add tomato, cucumber and radishes. Refrigerate until ready to serve. Toss salad with dressing of your choice.

SALAD DRESSINGS

CHEF'S SALAD DRESSING

⅔ c. sour cream
⅔ c. mayonnaise
Dash salt and pepper
1 t. onion, grated
1 t. lemon juice
3 dashes tabasco sauce

Combine all ingredients and mix well. Serve immediately or refrigerate. Makes 1½ cups.

OIL AND VINEGAR DRESSING

¼ c. salad oil
⅓ c. vinegar
1 t. salt
¼ c. sugar

Combine all ingredients in a jar; mix well before serving. Makes ½ cup.

BACON DRESSING

8 slices bacon
½ c. vinegar
½ t. sugar
   Salt and pepper to taste

Chop bacon into small pieces and fry until crispy. Remove from heat and stir in vinegar a little at a time. Add sugar, salt and pepper, stirring constantly. Return to heat for 1-2 minutes, then pour over salad. Makes ½ cup.

BLUE CHEESE DRESSING

½ c. salad oil
1 t. salt
¼ c. vinegar
¼ t. pepper
3 T. crumbled blue cheese
½ t. sugar

Combine all ingredients in a jar; mix well. Refrigerate and shake well before serving. Makes ¾ cup.

THOUSAND ISLAND DRESSING

½ c. mayonnaise
¼ c. chili sauce
¼ t. Worcestershire sauce
¼ t. salt
⅛ t. paprika
1 hard-boiled egg, finely chopped
1 t. green pepper, minced
2 t. pimiento, minced
½ t. onion juice

Mix all ingredients together and chill. Makes 1 cup.

ITALIAN DRESSING

½ c. salad oil
1 t. salt
¼ t. pepper
¼ t. garlic salt
¼ t. oregano
¼ c. lemon juice
2 T. chopped onion

Combine all ingredients and mix well. Refrigerate and shake well before serving. Makes ¾ cups.

ROQUEFORT DRESSING

½ c. salad oil
2 T. wine vinegar
2 T. lemon juice
½ t. salt
½ t. celery seed
   Dash pepper
½ t. sugar
⅓ c. Roquefort cheese, crumbled

Combine all ingredients in a jar; mix well. Refrigerate. Shake well before serving. Makes 1 cup.

Wash salad greens and drain well before storing in crisper drawer of refrigerator.

FRENCH DRESSING

½ c. salad oil
¼ c. vinegar
1 T. sugar
1 t. grated onion
1 t. salt
   Dash pepper
   Dash paprika
¼ c. catsup

Combine all ingredients and mix well. Refrigerate and shake well before serving. Makes ¾ cups.

CHEF SALAD

A chef salad and summertime
Are naturals together;
They're cool to eat and fun to serve
In time of torrid weather.

If you are quite a gardener,
Then you have right at hand,
The bulk of the ingredients
That make this salad grand.

Just start with lettuce cool and crisp,
And add a touch of these:
Fresh carrot curls and radishes
And bits of ham and cheese.

Remember, though, that you're the chef,
So add what you may wish.
I think some cukes and onion rings
Help liven up the dish.

Then garnish with hard-boiled egg
And dressing of your choice,
And you've a one-dish salad meal
To make your guests rejoice!

Craig E. Sathoff

THREE-BEAN SALAD

1 small can cut green beans
1 small can cut yellow wax beans
1 small can kidney beans
¼ c. green pepper, diced
¼ c. onion, diced
¼ t. salt
6 T. sugar
¼ t. pepper
¼ c. vinegar
¼ c. salad oil

Drain liquid from beans. Place in a bowl and mix with green pepper and onion. Add remaining ingredients and mix well. Keep refrigerated until ready to serve.

Salad is best if prepared at least a day before serving.

CUCUMBER SALAD

1 large cucumber, peeled and sliced
½ t. salt
½ c. sour cream
1 T. lemon juice
½ T. onion, chopped
⅛ t. sugar
   Dash pepper

Combine sour cream, lemon juice, salt, onion, sugar and pepper in a small bowl. Add cucumber to sour cream mixture and toss until well coated. Refrigerate until ready to serve.

Flute cucumber slices by pulling fork firmly down length of cucumber. Continue around cucumber. Slice.

SUMMER SALAD

1 pkg. lemon gelatin
1 c. hot water
¾ c. cold water
1 T. salt
1 T. vinegar
1 c. diced tomatoes
2 T. green pepper, chopped
2 T. onion, chopped

Add hot water to gelatin, stirring to dissolve. Add cold water. Refrigerate until it starts to thicken. Add tomato, green pepper and onion. Serve after gelatin hardens.

HINT: 6-7 ice cubes may be used instead of ¾ cups water to speed chilling of gelatin. After adding ice, stir until gelatin thickens (about 3 minutes). Remove ice cubes that have not melted.

Pictured opposite
Three-Bean Salad

SOUPS

CREAM OF MUSHROOM SOUP

⅓ c. mushrooms   ½ c. cream
3 T. butter   Dash salt
1⅓ c. chicken stock   Dash pepper
2 egg yolks

Melt butter in a medium saucepan. Add mushrooms and cook until tender. Remove from heat and cool. Add to chicken stock; mix together in electric blender until mushrooms are chopped. Blend in egg yolks. Pour mixture back into saucepan; add cream, stirring until mixture is thickened. Season with salt and pepper to taste.

CHEESE MUSHROOM SOUP

2 T. butter
2 t. fresh lemon juice
¼ lb. fresh mushrooms, sliced
1 small onion, chopped
1 T. all-purpose flour
2 t. chicken stock base
¼ t. dill weed
2 c. milk
1 egg, slightly beaten
¾ c. (3 ozs.) shredded cheddar cheese

Melt butter in a 1-quart saucepan; add lemon juice, mushrooms and onion. Sauté until onions are tender. Stir in flour, chicken stock base and dill. Cook over low heat until mixture is smooth. Remove from heat. Stir in milk. Heat to boiling, stirring constantly. Boil 1 minute stirring constantly. Blend a small amount of hot mixture into egg; return all to pan. Cook 1 minute. Remove from heat; stir in cheese until melted. If necessary, return to low heat to finish melting cheese. Do not boil. Makes 3 cups.

Cheese Mushroom Soup

CLAM CHOWDER

1 slice bacon
2 T. diced onion
¼ t. salt
    Dash pepper
1 8-oz. can minced clams
1 c. milk
1 T. butter
½ c. water
1 small potato, pared and diced

Sauté bacon until crisp in a small saucepan. Add onion and cook until tender. Add potatoes to water, and season with salt and pepper. Cook until potatoes are tender. Add clams with liquid, milk and butter. Cook for 3 minutes. Simmer, until ready to serve.

TOMATO SOUP

1 T. butter
2 onions, sliced
2 large tomatoes, peeled
1 c. chicken broth
¾ T. lemon juice
1 t. sugar
½ t. salt
   Dash pepper

Add onions and tomatoes to melted butter and simmer until tender. Add remaining ingredients; bring to a boil and simmer until ready to serve.

MINESTRONE

1 T. butter
¾ c. frozen mixed vegetables
½ qt. boiling water
   Dash thyme
½ t. salt
   Dash pepper
¼ c. macaroni

Sauté vegetables in melted butter in a medium saucepan until tender. Add remaining ingredients and boil for 5 minutes. Reduce heat and simmer for 30 minutes or until ready to serve.

FRENCH ONION SOUP

2 T. butter
2 c. sliced onion
2 10½-oz. cans beef bouillon
½ t. salt
2 slices toasted French bread
   Dash pepper
1 T. parmesan cheese

In large skillet, sauté onion in melted butter until tender. Mix bouillon, onion and salt and bring to a boil in a medium saucepan. Reduce heat, and simmer. Pour over French bread, and top with parmesan cheese. For best flavor, allow to sit a day before serving.

CHICKEN SOUP

2 c. chicken stock
¼ c. cooked chicken, chopped
1 T. diced pimiento
2 T. uncooked rice
   Salt
   Pepper

Heat chicken stock; add chicken, pimiento, and rice and bring to a boil. Reduce heat; simmer covered for 15 minutes. Season with salt and pepper.

HAMBURGER SOUP

½ lb. ground beef
3 c. boiling water
1 c. tomato juice
¼ c. shredded carrots
1 c. diced potatoes
¼ c. chopped celery
2 T. uncooked rice
1 medium onion, chopped
1 t. salt

Cook beef; add remaining ingredients, and simmer for 30 minutes or until vegetables are tender.

Mrs. Margaret Weiss

POTATO SOUP

2 medium-sized potatoes, pared and diced
2 slices onion
1 t. salt
1 c. hot milk
   Dash pepper
1 stalk celery, sliced very fine
⅓ c. water

Combine potatoes, onion and salt in a saucepan; add boiling water. Cover and cook until potatoes are tender. Do not drain. Mash potatoes with a fork; add milk, pepper, and celery. More milk may be added if soup is too thick. Serve hot.

AMOUNTS TO BUY
FOR TWO SERVINGS

FRESH VEGETABLES:

Asparagus—1 lb.
Beans, green or wax—½ to ¾ lb.
Broccoli—1 lb.
Cabbage—½ lb. if served raw
Carrots—½ lb.
Greens—1 lb.
Peas—1 to 1½ lbs.
Sweet or white potatoes—¾ to 1 lb.

MEDIUM WHITE SAUCE
FOR VEGETABLES

2 T. butter	Dash pepper
2 T. flour	1 c. milk
½ t. salt	

In a medium saucepan, melt butter and re-move from heat. Add flour, salt and pepper stirring until smooth. Gradually stir in milk. Return to stove and bring to a boil over medium heat, stirring constantly. Reduce heat and simmer for one minute.

THIN WHITE SAUCE

Follow the same recipe as the one used for medium white sauce. Amount of butter and flour should be reduced to 1 tablespoon each.

THICK WHITE SAUCE

Follow the same recipe as the one used for medium white sauce. Amount of butter should be increased to 3 tablespoons and the flour should be increased to 3 to 4 table-spoons.

GREEN PEAS WITH
PEARL ONIONS

2 T. butter	1 10-oz. pkg. frozen
½ c. pearl onions	peas
Dash pepper	½ t. salt

Melt butter in medium fry pan. Add peas and onions. Cook, covered, until peas are tender, about 15 minutes.

CHEESE-BACON
STUFFED TOMATOES

2 medium tomatoes
6 bacon slices
¼ c. green pepper, chopped
¼ c. onion, chopped
¾ c. shredded cheddar cheese
1 T. lettuce, chopped
1 T. crushed cheese crackers
2 t. butter

Cut thin slice from top of each tomato; scoop out pulp and set aside. Drain tomatoes up-side down on rack. Meanwhile, in a skillet, cook bacon until almost done. Drain off fat. Add pepper and onion; sauté until soft. Re-move skillet from heat and blend in cheese, lettuce and tomato pulp. Fill each shell with half of mixture. Sprinkle with cracker crumbs and dot each with 1 teaspoon butter. Place in buttered baking dish. Bake in pre-heated 400° oven 25 to 30 minutes.

Pictured opposite
Cheese-Bacon Stuffed Tomatoes

ACORN SQUASH

1 acorn squash   Pepper
2 T. butter   2 t. brown sugar
  Salt

Halve squash and remove seeds. Arrange squash in a small casserole, cut side up. Dab each cavity with butter and season with salt and pepper. Add brown sugar to each half. Bake in preheated 350° oven 45 minutes.

OVEN FRIED POTATOES

 2 medium potatoes
 3 T. butter
¼ t. salt
⅛ t. white pepper
  Paprika

Pare and slice potatoes in round slices ⅛ inch thick. Butter 1-quart casserole. Add layers of overlapping potato slices. Dot each layer with butter; season with salt and pepper. Sprinkle with paprika. Cover casserole. Bake in preheated 400° oven 30 minutes. Uncover; bake 10 minutes.

SWEET-SOUR CARROTS

1¼ c. carrots
  2 T. vegetable oil
  1 T. vinegar
¼ c. sugar
¼ t. mustard
¼ t. Worcestershire sauce
  1 8-oz. can tomato sauce
  1 T. diced onion

Slice carrots; cook in salted water. When tender, drain carrots. Combine remaining ingredients and add to carrots. Reheat. Serve hot.

ASPARAGUS WITH MUSHROOM SAUCE

1 10-oz. pkg. frozen asparagus spears
½ 10½-oz. can condensed cream of
   mushroom soup

Cook asparagus according to directions on package. Heat soup. Drain asparagus; turn into serving dish. Pour soup over asparagus.

SAVORY BROILED TOMATOES

2 small tomatoes
Melted butter
Salt and pepper
Fine dry bread crumbs
Grated cheese

Cut tomatoes in half. Place in shallow baking dish. Brush cut surfaces with melted butter. Sprinkle with salt and pepper. Broil until tomato halves begin to soften and brown. Sprinkle with crumbs and grated cheese and continue to broil until lightly browned.

Variations: Garlic salt and favorite herbs may be used instead of salt and pepper. A mixture of equal parts dairy sour cream and mayonnaise seasoned with curry powder to taste may be used instead of bread crumbs and cheese.

FRUITED RICE

⅔ c. rice
1 8-oz. can fruit cocktail
1 T. butter

Cook rice according to package directions. Drain fruit cocktail and add to rice. Stir in butter and simmer until ready to serve.

White rice triples in volume when cooked.

WILD RICE

1 c. wild rice
1 t. salt
¾ c. cooked mushrooms, chopped

Wash rice and drain. Combine rice and salt with 6 cups cold water in a large saucepan. Cover and bring to a boil. Uncover and boil for 50 minutes or until rice is tender. Drain rice and return to saucepan. Add mushrooms and simmer 10 to 15 minutes.

RICE PARISIAN

1¼ c. water
1 T. butter
⅓ c. uncooked rice
¼ c. mushrooms
½ pkg. dried onion soup

Melt butter in medium saucepan. Add mushrooms and rice; sauté until brown. Add soup and water; simmer covered for 30 minutes.

SPANISH RICE

2 slices bacon
⅓ c. white rice
1 t. instant minced onion
2 T. minced celery
2 T. minced green pepper
½ t. salt
⅛ t. pepper
2 c. stewed tomatoes

Place diced bacon in 8-inch skillet; cook slowly until bacon is crisp. Add washed and drained rice, onion, celery, green pepper, salt, pepper and tomatoes; mix well. Bring to boil. Cover skillet; cook over low heat 35 minutes stirring occasionally.

A KITCHEN PRAYER

God bless my little kitchen,
I love its every nook,
And God bless me as I do my work,
Wash pots and pans and cook.

And may the meals that I prepare
Be successful from above;
With Thy blessing and Thy grace
But most of all Thy love.

As we partake of earthly good
The table before us spread,
We'll not forget to thank Thee, Lord,
Who gives us daily bread.

So bless my little kitchen, Lord,
And those who enter in.
May they find naught but joy and peace
And happiness therein.

Margaret Petersen

BAKED POTATOES IN FOIL

2 small baking potatoes
2 T. butter
  Sour Cream Topping

Scrub potatoes; dry. Wrap in foil. Place on oven rack. Bake in 400° oven 1 to 1¼ hours. Remove from oven. Push back or remove foil. Cut 1½ inch slits in center of potatoes lengthwise and crosswise. Push ends of potatoes toward center to open slightly. Place 1 tablespoon butter in each potato. Serve with Sour Cream Topping.

SOUR CREAM TOPPING

  ¼ t. salt
1½ t. onion juice
  ⅛ t. white pepper
  ¼ t. Worcestershire sauce
  1 t. chopped chives
  ½ c. sour cream

Add seasonings and chives to sour cream; mix well. Makes enough for 2 medium potatoes.

FLOWER POTATOES

2 potatoes
  Butter
  Salt
  Pepper

Peel potatoes. Slice through potato almost to underside, brush potato with butter and sprinkle with salt, pepper, and other desired seasonings. Wrap loosely in aluminum foil. Bake in a preheated 350° oven 1 hour or until tender. Potatoes open like flowers when done. Grated cheese may be sprinkled on top of potatoes after baking for added flavor. Allow cheese to melt by placing under broiler.

DILLED POTATO SALAD WITH WURST

  2 large potatoes
1½ c. boiling water
  2 slices bacon, cut-up
  1 small onion, chopped
  1 stalk celery, chopped
  ¼ c. chopped dill pickles
  ½ lb. knackwurst or frankfurters
  ½ c. dill pickle liquid (drained from dill pickles)
  2 t. sugar
  ¼ t. caraway seed
  ¼ t. dry mustard
  ¼ t. salt
  1 T. chopped parsley

Cook unpeeled potatoes in boiling water until partially tender, about 10 to 15 minutes. Peel potatoes and cut into thick slices. In large skillet over medium heat, cook bacon until partially cooked. Add onion, celery and pickles; cook, stirring occasionally, until onion and celery are tender, about 3 to 5 minutes. Stir in potatoes, knackwurst, pickle liquid, sugar, caraway seed, dry mustard and salt. Cover and cook over low heat, turning potatoes occasionally with pancake turner, until potatoes are tender and knackwurst is heated through, about 10 minutes. To serve, spoon potato mixture into a bowl; top with knackwurst. Garnish with parsley.

NOTE: Knackwurst may be cooked separately in skillet, broiler or over charcoal grill, if desired.

> Store onions, potatoes and all root vegetables in cool, dry, well-ventilated place.

CASSEROLES

A LOVELY RECIPE

My mother often spoke to me
About a lovely recipe,
Where many good ingredients
Enriched with faith and diligence,
Would make a smoother life, and start
The joy expanding in a heart:
She said, "Sometimes a bit of spice
(That should be tested once . . . or twice,
To be assured it won't offend
The taste of stranger, foe, or friend),
Enhances friendliness and fun
Within the heart, of anyone,
Where warmth is kept, in readiness
To start the effort toward success,
With something very fine, and good
Enough to serve the neighborhood—"
And, life is helping me to see
The beauty of the recipe.

Bessie Trull Law

BROCCOLI CASSEROLE WITH NOODLES

    4 oz. noodles
1½ T. butter
    ¼ t. salt
        Dash pepper
    1 bunch broccoli, cleaned and cooked
    ½ c. sliced mushrooms
    1 c. cooked chicken, sliced
    1 c. sour cream

Cook noodles as package directs. In melted butter mix salt and pepper with noodles. In a separate dish mix cooked broccoli with mushrooms. Combine chicken with sour cream. In a small casserole dish, arrange half of noodles; add meat mixture, and broccoli. Top with rest of noodles. Bake in a 350° oven for 30 minutes.

MACARONI COMBINATION CASSEROLE

    1 c. macaroni (uncooked)
    ⅛ lb. shredded cheese
    ⅛ lb. ground ham
    1 can cream of mushroom soup
    2 eggs, hard boiled
    1 T. onion, diced

Combine all ingredients and place in a small casserole. Let stand overnight. Bake for 1 hour in a 350° oven.

POTATO-TOPPED BEEF CASSEROLE

    1 T. shortening
    1 small onion, thinly sliced
    1 stalk celery, chopped
    ½ green pepper, chopped
    1 small bay leaf
    ⅓ c. catsup
    ¾ c. water
    ¼ t. sugar
    ½ t. salt
    ⅛ t. pepper
    ¼ t. Worcestershire sauce
2⅓ to 3 c. cooked beef, cubed
    ½ c. cooked carrots
    1 c. mashed potatoes (leftover or instant)
    1 T. melted butter

Melt shortening in 10-inch skillet. Add onion, celery, green pepper and bay leaf. Cook 8 minutes. Pour in catsup and water; stir until blended. Heat until mixture bubbles. Remove from heat. Season with sugar, salt, pepper and Worcestershire sauce. Remove bay leaf. Add beef and carrots. Mix well. Pour into two 1¼-cup casseroles. Squeeze mashed potatoes through pastry bag over top of casserole. Drip melted butter over potatoes. Bake in preheated 350° oven 20 to 25 minutes.

SCALLOPED POTATOES

1 c. cream of mushroom soup
¼ c. grated cheddar cheese
2 c. potatoes, sliced
½ t. salt
⅓ c. milk
2 T. onion, diced

Combine soup, cheese, onion, salt and milk in small casserole. Add potatoes and mix. Bake in preheated 375° oven for 1 hour.

YAM SOUFFLÉ

1 16-oz. can sweet potatoes
1 c. granulated sugar
2 eggs
¾ stick butter
1 c. milk
½ t. nutmeg
1 t. cinnamon

Heat sweet potatoes and granulated sugar in a medium saucepan. Remove from heat. Mix eggs, melted butter, milk, nutmeg and cinnamon together. Add to potato and sugar mixture and place in casserole. Bake in preheated 400° oven 20 minutes.

TOPPING

6 T. cornflakes, crushed
¼ c. pecans, chopped
6 T. butter
¼ c. brown sugar

Heat cornflakes, pecans, brown sugar and butter together. Pour over top of casserole; bake additional 10 minutes.

SWEET POTATO CASSEROLE

8 oz. sweet potatoes
1 T. light brown sugar
⅛ t. allspice
1 T. butter
½ t. lemon juice

Slice potatoes and layer in a small casserole. Sprinkle each layer with sugar, butter, allspice, and lemon juice. Bake in a preheated 400° oven for 20 minutes.

BEEF AND RICE CASSEROLE

½ lb. ground beef
½ c. quick-cooking rice
½ pkg. frozen peas
1 can tomato soup, diluted
½ t. salt
   Dash pepper
2 T. chopped onion

Brown ground beef with onion. Combine uncooked rice, peas, soup diluted with one can water and spices. Bake in a preheated 325° oven for 1 hour.

HAMBURGER-TATER HOT DISH

½ lb. ground beef
½ small onion, chopped
1 c. cream of mushroom soup
2 T. water
1 c. Tater Tots

Brown hamburger and onion. Add soup to water. Pour over hamburger and onion in a shallow baking dish. Top with frozen Tater Tots. Bake at 350° for 20 to 30 minutes.

Mrs. Clarence T. Malmquist

CHILI CHEESE SOUFFLÉ

¼ lb. (1 c.) sharp cheddar cheese, shredded
4 oz. mild green chilies
1 egg, separated
½ T. flour
½ t. salt

Layer chilies and cheese in bottom of greased baking pan. Beat egg whites until stiff; fold in lightly beaten egg yolks, flour and salt. Spread over layered ingredients. Bake in a preheated 350° oven 30 minutes. Serve hot.

ENCHILADA CASSEROLE

½ lb. ground beef
1 8-oz. can tomato sauce
½ c. water
½ T. chili powder
¼ t. ground cumin
¼ t. salt
4 corn or flour tortillas
  Pure vegetable oil
1 c. shredded sharp cheddar cheese
¼ c. chopped green onions
2 T. green peppers, sliced
½ c. dairy sour cream (optional)

Brown beef in a medium saucepan. Remove from heat and drain fat. Stir in tomato sauce, water, chili powder, cumin and salt. Heat oil in a small saucepan; add tortillas and fry one at a time, softened and puffed. Drain on paper towels. In a small baking dish, arrange in layers; tortilla, meat sauce, onions, cheese and green peppers, reserving ⅛ cup cheese for top. Repeat layers until all tortillas are used. Sprinkle reserved cheese on top. Bake uncovered in a preheated 350° oven 20 to 25 minutes. Serve hot. Cut in wedges and garnish with sour cream.

HAM AND CAULIFLOWER CASSEROLE

1 small cauliflower, separated
¼ c. cornflake crumbs
¼ lb. cooked diced ham
3 T. chopped green pepper
½ c. shredded cheddar cheese
¾ c. sour cream
¼ c. grated parmesan cheese
  Dash paprika

Add cauliflower to water. Boil 15 minutes or until tender; mix with crumbs. Add ham, green pepper and cheddar cheese. Place mixture in buttered casserole dish. Pour sour cream over top. Sprinkle with parmesan cheese. Bake in a preheated 325° oven 20 minutes.

SAVORY NOODLES AND MUSHROOMS

1 T. butter
2 c. cooked beef, cubed
1 medium onion, chopped
1 small clove garlic, minced
1 4-oz. can mushrooms, undrained
1 c. canned tomatoes
¼ c. sliced ripe olives
¼ t. salt
¼ t. thyme
⅛ t. pepper
2 c. cooked noodles
½ c. (2 oz.) shredded cheddar cheese

Melt butter in skillet. Add meat and onion. Cook until onions are golden. Add remaining ingredients. Toss together lightly. Turn into greased 1-quart casserole. Bake in preheated 350° oven 15 to 20 minutes.

Ham and Cauliflower Casserole

POTATOES AU GRATIN

2 T. butter
2½ T. onion, chopped
¼ c. milk
6 oz. condensed cheddar cheese soup
2 T. fine, dry, bread crumbs
2 c. cooked, cubed potatoes
2½ T. chopped pimiento

Sauté onion in 1 tablespoon melted butter until tender. Mix together cheese soup and milk. Melt remaining butter and mix with bread crumbs. In a casserole dish, arrange potatoes, soup mixture and pimiento in layers. Top with bread crumbs. Bake in a preheated 375° oven for 30 minutes.

CHILI SKILLET MEAL

2 slices bacon, halved
1 small onion, sliced
½ green pepper, diced
1 1-lb. can kidney beans
½ c. chili sauce
2 t. chili powder
¼ t. salt
⅛ t. pepper
2 ozs. sharp cheddar cheese, grated
½ lb. frankfurters, sliced
2 large English muffins, halved and lightly toasted

Heat skillet over moderate heat for 3 minutes; add bacon. Cook 2 minutes on each side. Drain. Add onion and green pepper to fat in skillet. Cook until lightly browned, about 4 minutes. Add kidney beans. Reduce heat. Crumble bacon and add with remaining ingredients except muffins, stirring until cheese is melted; cover and heat thoroughly. Serve on muffins.

QUICK BAKED BEANS

⅛ lb. salt pork
1 1-lb. can baked beans (with tomato sauce)
1 T. brown sugar
1 T. molasses
3 T. catsup
1 t. instant minced onions
¼ t. dry mustard

Cut salt pork in slices. Place in saucepan, cover with cold water and bring to boil. Drain. Pan-fry salt pork until golden brown, about 5 minutes. Place beans, brown sugar, molasses, catsup, onion and dry mustard in a saucepan; bring to boil. Turn bean mixture into two individual 1¼-cup casseroles; top with salt pork. Bake in 350° oven 40 to 45 minutes.

TUNA IN TOAST CUPS

2 stalks celery, thinly sliced
1 medium onion, chopped
½ green pepper, chopped
Butter
1 pkg. white sauce mix
8 ozs. American cheese, cubed
1 7-oz. can tuna, drained and flaked
2 T. chopped pimiento
Toast Cups

Cook celery, onion and green peppers in butter until tender. Prepare sauce mix as directed on package. Stir in celery, onion, green pepper, cheese, tuna and pimiento; heat until cheese melts. Serve in Toast Cups.

TOAST CUPS

Heat oven to 375°. Trim crusts from thinly sliced fresh bread; spread with soft butter. Press buttered side down into muffin cups. Bake 12 minutes or until lightly toasted.

NOTE: 1 cup cooked, cubed chicken or turkey may be substituted for tuna.

Quick Baked Beans

TUNA CASSEROLE

1 c. macaroni
1 t. salt
½ c. sharp cheddar cheese, shredded
¼ c. butter
¾ c. milk
½ c. onion, chopped
¼ c. celery, chopped
2 T. butter
1 can cream of mushroom soup
1 6½-oz. can tuna

Add macaroni and salt to 1 quart rapidly boiling water. Boil 7 to 10 minutes, stirring occasionally. Drain and return to pan. Add butter, milk and cheese; mix well. Sauté onion and celery in melted butter until tender. Add to macaroni with remaining ingredients; mix well. Pour into small casserole dish. Bake in preheated 350° oven 30 minutes.

TASTY SALMON CASSEROLE

1 10-oz. can condensed cream of
  celery soup
½ c. salad dressing
¼ c. milk
¼ c. grated parmesan cheese
1 10-oz. pkg. frozen peas, cooked
1 1-lb. can salmon, drained, flaked
4 ozs. cooked noodles
1 T. onion, chopped

Combine soup, salad dressing, milk and cheese; blend well. Stir in peas, salmon, noodles and onion; mix lightly. Pour into two 1½-pint casseroles; bake in 350° oven about 20 minutes. Serve one casserole immediately. Allow other casserole to cool; cover with foil and freeze for later use. Serve 2, freeze 2.

To keep salt dry for easy pouring, put a few grains of rice into shaker.

BREADED PORK CHOPS

4 center cut pork chops
½ c. flour
1 t. seasoned salt
⅛ t. pepper
1 egg
2 T. milk
½ c. fine dry bread crumbs
2 T. shortening
¼ c. chicken broth or water

Dip chops in flour mixed with salt and pepper; then in egg slightly beaten with 2 tablespoons milk. Dip chops in bread crumbs. Heat shortening in skillet 3 minutes. Add pork chops; brown 3 minutes on each side. Add broth. Cover; cook over medium heat 45 minutes or until chops are tender. Take cover off skillet for the last 5 minutes. Remove chops to serving platter.

AMOUNTS TO BUY
FOR TWO SERVINGS

MEAT:

Ground beef—½ to ⅔ lb.
Roasts—3 to 4 lbs. (2 to 3 meals)
Pot Roast—2 to 3 lbs.
Chops—2 to 4 depending on size
Spareribs—2 lbs.
Sausage—½ to ⅔ lb.
Smoked ham—1 slice ¾-inch thick
Frankfurters—½ lb.
Liver—½ lb.

VEGETABLE STUFFED ROUND STEAK

3 lbs. round steak, cut thin
½ t. seasoned salt
½ c. flour
¼ c. chopped green pepper
¼ c. shredded carrots
⅓ c. chopped celery
2 T. minced onion
1 4-oz. can mushroom pieces
½ t. salt
1 T. vegetable oil
1 c. beef broth
1 T. catsup
Pinch sugar

Remove bone from steak; cut steak in 6 strips. Combine salt and flour; pound into meat. Mix together green pepper, carrots, celery, onion, mushroom pieces and salt. Divide evenly and spread filling over half of each meat strip. Roll up meat. Tie with string. Heat skillet 3 minutes. Add oil; brown meat on all sides, about 5 minutes. Add broth, catsup and sugar; cover. Simmer 1 hour or until meat is tender.

GRAVY

1 c. beef broth
¼ c. flour
¼ c. cold water

Add beef broth to skillet; bring to boil. Make a paste of cold water and flour. Add to skillet, stirring constantly. Simmer 10 minutes; stir occasionally. Makes 1 cup gravy.

Pictured opposite
Vegetable Stuffed Round Steak

BAKED CHICKEN AND RICE

⅔ c. quick-cooking rice
1 can cream of chicken soup
3-4 pieces chicken
½ envelope onion soup mix

Mix together rice and cream of chicken soup. Spread on bottom of casserole. Lay pieces of chicken on top. Sprinkle with onion soup mix. Cover tightly and bake in preheated 325° oven 1½ hours.

Sis Dennison

LAMB CURRY

1 c. rice
1 c. cubed leftover lamb
¼ t. curry powder
2 T. onion, chopped
2 T. green pepper, chopped
1 c. leftover gravy
⅛ t. salt
¼ c. apple, peeled and diced

Cook rice as package directs. Sauté onion, and green pepper until tender. Add remaining ingredients, stirring as mixture comes to a boil. Reduce heat, cover and simmer until apple is tender. Serve over rice.

PORK CHOP SUEY

2 t. salad oil
⅓ c. onion, chopped
⅔ c. celery, chopped
3 T. leftover gravy
¼ c. cream of mushroom soup
1 T. soy sauce
½ c. sliced roast pork
½ c. drained bean sprouts
1 t. cornstarch
1 c. cooked rice

Sauté onion and celery in hot oil, until onion is tender. Add soup, soy sauce, and gravy, stirring as mixture comes to a boil. Add pork and bean sprouts, bring to a boil. Reduce heat and simmer covered. Stir cornstarch and water together until smooth. Add to pork mixture. Cook, stirring constantly until mixture boils and becomes thick. Serve over rice.

VEAL STEAKS WITH TOMATO SAUCE

1 T. butter	¼ c. water
¼ c. chopped onion	⅛ t. salt
2 veal steaks	Dash pepper
4 oz. tomato juice	⅛ t. oregano

Sauté onions in melted butter; remove from pan. Add meat and brown on both sides. Add onions, tomato juice, water, oregano, salt and pepper; simmer until tender, about 1 hour.

BROILED LAMB CHOPS

2 loin lamb chops	Salt
(1 inch thick)	Pepper
1 t. lemon juice	Lemon wedges
½ t. oregano	Parsley

Brush one side of chops with lemon juice; sprinkle with oregano. Broil chops 6 to 8 minutes on one side. Season with salt and pepper. Turn; brush second side with lemon juice; sprinkle with oregano. Broil 6 to 8 minutes. Season with salt and pepper. Garnish with lemon wedges and parsley. For additional flavor, squeeze lemon wedges over cooked chops.

BARBECUED SPARERIBS

1 T. cornstarch
⅓ c. dark corn syrup
3 T. soy sauce
1½ t. ground ginger
2 T. vinegar
1 clove garlic, crushed
2 lbs. meaty spareribs or backribs
Salt
Pepper

To prepare marinade, combine cornstarch, syrup, soy sauce, ginger, vinegar and garlic. Cut spareribs into serving pieces and place in single layer in shallow dish. Pour marinade over meat; refrigerate four hours or overnight. Remove spareribs from marinade; season with salt and pepper. Place in shallow baking dish; cover with aluminum foil. Bake in 350° oven 1½ hours. Remove foil. Broil five inches from heat. Turn once and baste frequently with sauce.

Rock Lobster Supreme

ROCK LOBSTER SUPREME

4 4-oz. frozen South African rock lobster
  tails
¼ c. consommé
1 small onion, chopped
½ lb. mushrooms, trimmed and sliced
⅓ c. dry sherry
2 T. cornstarch
1 egg yolk
1½ c. milk
½ t. dry mustard
¼ t. tabasco sauce
1 t. paprika
  Salt

Drop frozen rock lobster tails into boiling salted water. When water reboils, parboil for 2 minutes. Drain and drench with cold water. With scissors, remove underside membrane and pull out meat in one piece. Dice meat, reserving shells for serving. In a saucepan, heat consommé and add onion and mushrooms. Stir over low heat until vegetables are tender. In a bowl, mix sherry, cornstarch and egg yolk. Add milk to vegetables and stir in cornstarch mixture. Add dry mustard, tabasco sauce and paprika. Stir over low heat until sauce bubbles and thickens. Add lobster and season to taste with salt. Use mixture to stuff reserved shells. Place under broiler and broil for 5 minutes or until bubbly.

CORNISH GAME HENS

2 (1-lb. size) Cornish Game Hens
½ t. salt
¼ t. pepper
6 T. butter
¼ lemon juice
⅛ t. paprika

Sprinkle salt and pepper in each hen. Truss hens: Bring skin over neck opening and fasten to back with metal pick. Tie legs together with string. Bend wings under bird. Close cavity with metal picks. Combine 4 tablespoons butter with lemon juice and paprika, stirring well to make basting sauce. Brown hens in remaining butter in medium skillet. Put hens in large roasting pan, without rack; brush with basting sauce. Roast in a preheated 450° oven 40 minutes or until tender. Garnish each hen with a crab apple.

CHICKEN A LA KING

2 oz. mushrooms
¼ c. chopped green pepper
¼ c. butter
¼ c. flour
   Scant ½ t. salt
⅛ t. pepper
1 c. chicken broth
1 c. cream (20% butterfat)
1 c. diced cooked chicken
¼ c. chopped pimiento

Sauté mushrooms and green pepper in melted butter. Blend in flour and seasonings. Cook over low heat, stirring until mixture is smooth and bubbly. Remove from heat; slowly stir in broth and cream. Bring to a boil over low heat, stirring constantly. Reduce heat and add chicken and pimiento. Continue cooking until meat is heated through. Serve hot over noodles or rice. Serves 4.

Luella Rohlfing

BEEF STROGANOFF

1 slice roast beef, 1½ inches thick
1 4-oz. can mushrooms, drained
2 T. butter
1 small onion, minced
1½ t. flour
¾ t. cornstarch
½ c. beef broth
1 T. chili sauce
¼ t. dry mustard
2 T. dry sherry
¼ t. paprika
½ c. dairy sour cream
   Cooked white rice

Cut roast beef in thin strips, ¼ inch thick and 3 to 4 inches long. Heat 10-inch skillet over moderate heat 3 minutes. Add 1 tablespoon butter. Add onion; cook 3 minutes or until golden. Remove onion from pan; add remaining 1 tablespoon butter to pan. Stir in flour and cornstarch. Cook until mixture bubbles. Stir in beef broth, chili sauce, mustard, sherry and paprika. Cook, stirring constantly, until sauce thickens. Add meat, mushrooms and onion. Cover. Reduce heat to low. Simmer 10 minutes. Stir in sour cream gradually. Heat thoroughly. Serve on cooked rice.

CORNED BEEF AND CABBAGE

5-6 lb. corned-beef brisket
1 clove garlic
1 onion, halved
2 cloves
⅛ t. pepper
1 large head cabbage, cut into wedges

Place corned beef in a large saucepan and cover with water. Add remaining ingredients except cabbage. Bring to a boil. Reduce heat and simmer for 5 minutes. Continue to simmer covered until tender. Add cabbage and simmer until cabbage is thoroughly cooked, about 15 minutes. Remove corned beef and cabbage from pan. Slice beef just before serving. Serves 8.

Halibut Steaks with Vegetables

HALIBUT STEAKS WITH VEGETABLES

¾ lb. halibut steak
2 T. lemon juice
½ t. salt
1 small tomato, sliced
1 carrot, shredded
2 T. onion, chopped
Lemon wedges

Place halibut steak in a baking dish. Pour lemon juice and salt over fish, followed by mixture of tomato, carrot, and onion. Bake, covered for 25 to 30 minutes in a 350° oven. Remove from oven. Garnish with lemon if desired.

INDIVIDUAL BARBECUED MEAT LOAVES

½ c. soft bread crumbs
¼ c. milk
1 egg
2 t. Worcestershire sauce
1 t. salt
¼ t. poultry seasoning
⅛ t. pepper
⅛ t. dry mustard
2 T. celery, finely chopped
2 T. onion, finely chopped
¾ lb. lean ground beef
¼ lb. ground pork

Mix bread crumbs with milk, egg, Worcestershire sauce, salt, poultry seasoning, pepper, mustard, celery and onion. Beat together; add beef and pork. Mix thoroughly. Shape into 4 individual oblong loaves. Place in a shallow baking pan; allow one inch between loaves. Bake in 350° oven 30 minutes. Spoon barbecue sauce over meat loaves. Return to oven: bake 10 minutes.

BARBECUE SAUCE

⅓ c. tomato sauce
1 small clove garlic, minced
1 T. vegetable oil
1 T. dark corn syrup
1 T. vinegar
¼ t. salt
⅛ t. pepper
⅛ t. oregano

Combine all ingredients in a very small saucepan. Simmer 10 minutes.

NOTE: To freeze cooked individual meat loaves, allow to cool, then wrap securely in aluminum foil. To serve; thaw overnight in refrigerator, unwrap, heat.

To chop parsley, stuff sprigs into tall glass; snip with kitchen scissors.

HAMBURGER STROGANOFF

½ lb. ground beef
2 T. butter
2 T. sliced mushrooms
¼ c. chopped onion
¼ clove garlic, minced
½ t. salt
⅛ t. pepper
¼ t. Worcestershire sauce
1 T. flour
2½ T. chili sauce
6 T. sour cream
Spaghetti

Brown ground beef in half of the butter. Add remaining butter, mushrooms, onion, garlic, salt and pepper; sauté until onions are golden and tender. Add Worcestershire sauce. Stir in flour, then chili sauce. Just before serving, blend in sour cream. Serve hot over cooked spaghetti.

GROUND BEEF DINNER

¾ lbs. ground beef
½ c. onion, diced
2 T. green pepper, chopped
1 potato, sliced
½ c. celery, chopped
Dash salt
Dash pepper
1 c. canned tomatoes
2 slices American cheese
Butter

Brown ground beef in a medium saucepan. In a casserole alternate layers of ground beef and vegetables. Add salt and pepper to each layer. Top with tomatoes and cheese. Bake covered in preheated 350° oven 1½ hours.

Pork with Sauerkraut

SWEDISH MEATBALLS

¾ lb. ground beef 1½ t. flour
½ t. salt   ½ c. cream
 2 t. pepper   1 beef bouillon
¼ t. thyme   cube
⅓ c. butter

Mix ground meat with salt, pepper and thyme in a medium bowl. Shape into meatballs. Brown meatballs in melted butter, in a large frying pan. Place meatballs in a casserole dish. Remove drippings from pan leaving 1 tablespoon. Add flour and stir until smooth. Stir in cream along with ½ c. water and bring to a boil. Reduce heat. Add bouillon cube and simmer for 3 minutes. Pour over meatballs, cover and bake in a preheated 350° oven 25 minutes.

PORK WITH SAUERKRAUT

 1 T. butter
 2 T. brown sugar
 4 T. chopped onion
½ c. gravy
 1 8 oz. can sauerkraut
 1 t. caraway seed
¼ t. salt
 4 slices leftover roast pork

Combine butter with sugar in a large saucepan. Cook slowly over low heat; stir constantly until sugar is melted. Add onion and simmer covered for 5 minutes. Add gravy, sauerkraut, salt and caraway seed; bring to a boil, and stir. Add pork to sauerkraut, and simmer covered for 10 minutes.

STEAK AND ONIONS

2½ lbs. round steak
1 10½-oz. can cream of mushroom soup
2 onions, sliced
⅓ c. water

Brown meat on both sides; drain grease off of meat. Pour mixture of soup, water and onions over meat and simmer covered for 1½ hours.

PIZZA

PIZZA DOUGH

¼ c. lard or shortening
¼ c. milk, scalded
1 pkg. dry yeast
¼ c. warm water (110° to 115°)
1½ c. all-purpose flour
½ t. salt

Add lard to scalded milk and cool to lukewarm. Dissolve yeast in warm water; add to milk. Mix flour with salt; add milk mixture. Stir to blend; knead dough about 5 minutes. Place on a greased cookie sheet or round pizza pan. Twirl dough to grease top. Cover with a tea towel and let rise in a warm place until doubled. Prepare Pizza Topping. Punch down dough and pat to ⅛ to ¼-inch thickness. Bake in preheated 400° oven for 5 minutes. Remove from oven. Arrange topping on dough and bake for 15 minutes.

PIZZA TOPPING

¼ t. sweet basil
½ t. oregano
¼ t. salt
1 6-oz. can tomato paste
1 pepperoni link (½ lb.), thinly sliced
1 4-oz. can mushroom stems and pieces, chopped
1½ c. grated mozzarella cheese
½ c. grated parmesan cheese

Add basil, oregano and salt to tomato paste. Spread half of tomato mixture over dough. Top with half the meat, half the mushrooms and half the mozzarella cheese. Repeat layers. Sprinkle parmesan cheese on top.

PORK ROAST WITH BARBEQUE SAUCE

1 5-lb. loin pork roast
½ c. brown sugar
1 c. catsup
2 T. mustard
2 T. tarragon vinegar
1 T. Worcestershire sauce
½ t. salt

Roast pork in preheated 325° oven 3 to 3½ hours. Meat thermometer should reach 185° when thoroughly cooked. Combine remaining ingredients in medium saucepan; cook over low heat, stirring until sugar is dissolved. Baste with barbecue sauce after roast has cooked for 2 to 2½ hours. Continue to baste every 15 minutes until done. Serve with remaining sauce.

BROILED STEAK WITH MUSHROOM TOPPING

1-inch thick beef steak (T-bone, porterhouse, tenderloin, club, strip, sirloin, rib)
Salt
Pepper

Slash fat edge of steak to prevent curling during broiling. Broil steak 5 to 7 minutes on each side for rare, 8 to 9 minutes on each side for medium or 10 to 12 minutes on each side for well-done. Season first side with salt and pepper just before turning. Season second side when broiling is completed. Remove to hot platter. Serve with Mushroom Topping.

MUSHROOM TOPPING

½ lb. mushrooms
3 T. butter

Wash mushrooms; drain. Cut lengthwise in thin slices. Melt butter; add mushrooms. Cover; cook over low heat 3 minutes or until some juice has formed in pan. Uncover; continue cooking about 5 minutes.

STUFFED GREEN PEPPERS
ITALIANO

4 large green peppers
½ c. Italian dressing
1 medium onion, chopped
1 lb. lean ground beef
⅔ c. cooked rice
⅓ c. dry bread crumbs
3 T. grated parmesan cheese
2 T. chopped parsley
1 egg, well beaten
1 8-oz. can tomato sauce
¼ c. water

Wash peppers, remove stems and seeds; parboil in salted water. Drain. In large skillet, heat ¼ cup Italian dressing and sauté onion until transparent. Add meat and brown well. Stir in rice and allow mixture to cool slightly. Stir bread crumbs, cheese, parsley and egg into meat mixture. Stuff peppers with mixture. Place peppers in a greased baking dish. In small bowl, combine remaining Italian dressing with tomato sauce and water. Pour over peppers. Bake in preheated 350° oven 20 minutes or until peppers are tender. Serves 4.

NOTE: Peppers may be frozen before baking. Carefully wrap each stuffed pepper in a piece of plastic wrap or foil. Place in a plastic bag and seal tightly. Freeze. Before serving, allow peppers to thaw overnight in refrigerator. Remove wrapping and bake as above.

Stuffed Green Peppers Italiano

LASAGNE

3 oz. lasagne noodles
  Dash oregano
1 8-oz. can spaghetti sauce
  with meat
½ c. cottage cheese
3 oz. sliced mozzarella cheese
  Dash salt
  Dash pepper

Cook lasagne noodles as package directs. Add oregano, salt, and pepper to spaghetti sauce. Alternate layers of noodles, cottage cheese, mozzarella, and sauce. Bake in a preheated 375° oven 30 minutes.

CHICKEN LIVERS

½ to ¾ lb. chicken livers
¼ c. all-purpose flour
1 t. salt
⅛ t. pepper
1 t. oregano, crushed
2 T. vegetable oil
  Lemon juice

Dredge livers in flour mixed with salt, pepper and oregano. Heat oil in skillet. Add livers; fry 10 minutes, turning frequently. Squeeze fresh lemon juice over top before serving.

HAM AND CABBAGE ROLLS

4 slices boiled ham
2 T. onion, chopped
2 T. butter
3 T. flour
1½ c. milk
2 t. mustard
½ c. shredded Swiss cheese
⅔ c. bread crumbs
2 c. cooked cabbage

Spread ½ cup cooked cabbage on each ham slice, and roll up. Place in a medium baking dish. Sauté onion in melted butter. Add flour and stir until blended. Add milk and mustard; cook until mixture comes to a boil. Stir in cheese. Pour over ham and top with mixture of bread crumbs and butter. Bake in preheated 375° oven 25 to 30 minutes.

ITALIAN SPAGHETTI

2 T. vegetable oil
½ lb. lean ground beef
1 small clove garlic, minced
1 medium onion, minced
1 6-oz. can tomato paste
1¾ c. tomatoes and juice
½ t. Worcestershire sauce
½ t. sugar
¼ t. celery salt
½ t. salt
⅛ t. pepper
⅛ t. basil
½ t. oregano
⅛ t. thyme
⅓ lb. spaghetti
2 T. parmesan cheese

Place vegetable oil in 8-inch skillet; add ground beef, garlic and onion. Cook slowly until lightly browned, about 20 minutes, stirring occasionally. Add tomato paste, tomatoes and seasonings. Simmer until thickened, about 1 hour. Serve on hot, well-drained spaghetti. Sprinkle with parmesan cheese.

TO COOK SPAGHETTI: Add spaghetti and 1½ teaspoons salt, 1 tablespoon vegetable oil to 2 quarts boiling water. Cook 12 to 15 minutes. Drain in colander. Rinse drained spaghetti under hot running water to prevent stickiness.

CHEESY CHICKEN BAKE

2 lb. frying chicken, cut up
½ c. soft margarine
⅓ c. flour
1 t. paprika
½ t. salt
2¼ c. crushed cheese flavored corn puffs
  Dash white pepper

Thoroughly dry chicken pieces. In small mixer bowl, combine margarine, flour, paprika, and salt. Blend on medium speed until thoroughly mixed. Spread flour mixture on one side of chicken. Roll coated side in crushed cheese flavored corn puffs. Place chicken pieces in ungreased 13 x 9-inch baking pan, coated side up. Sprinkle with pepper. Bake in 400° oven for 60 to 65 minutes or until golden brown.

TIPS FOR USING DRIED HERBS

Herbs are leaves of plants. They are usually dried and crushed when used and may be used separately or blended together. Buy only small amounts at a time. A little herb goes a long way and they do lose their flavor in time. Store in small, tightly sealed containers.

HERB CHART

Basil

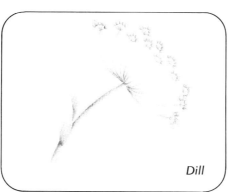
Dill

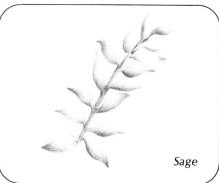
Marjoram

Oregano

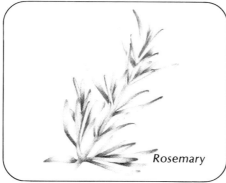
Rosemary

Sage

Savory

Tarragon

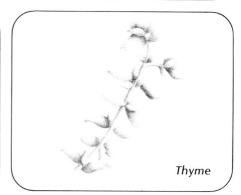
Thyme

HERBS	USE WITH:
Basil	Meat, fish, egg, cheese and tomato dishes.
Dill	Salads, soups and vegetable dishes.
Marjoram	Stews, soups, poultry, fish or lamb dishes.
Oregano	Salads, egg, meat and tomato dishes.
Rosemary	Stews, soups, fish, lamb, beef and potato dishes.
Sage	Poultry, meat, stews and cheese dishes.
Savory	Meat, poultry, dressings and sauces.
Tarragon	Sauces, salads, poultry, meat, eggs and tomato dishes.
Thyme	Soups, stews, meats, eggs and tomato dishes.

tured opposite
ian Spaghetti, page 37

 DESSERTS

GINGERBREAD

⅓ c. shortening
½ c. sugar
2 eggs
½ c. molasses
½ c. buttermilk
2 c. sifted cake flour
1 t. baking soda
1 t. ginger
½ t. cinnamon
¼ t. salt

Cream shortening. Add sugar; cream again. Beat in eggs, one at a time, beating well after each addition. Add molasses and buttermilk; mix well. Sift together remaining ingredients. Fold into first mixture. Pour into greased and floured 9 x 9 x 1¾-inch pan. Bake in preheated 350° oven 35 to 40 minutes. Serve plain or with whipped cream.

> 1 cup buttermilk or sour milk equals 1 tablespoon lemon juice plus milk to make 1 cup. Let stand 5 minutes.

SPICED APPLESAUCE

2 lb. cooking apples
½ c. sugar
½ t. cinnamon
Dash nutmeg
1 t. lemon juice

Core and pare apples, quarter. In a medium saucepan bring ½ cup water to a boil. Add apples and bring to a boil. Reduce heat. Cover and simmer 20 to 25 minutes, stirring occasionally. Water may be added if needed. Add rest of ingredients, stirring until combined. Applesauce may be served warm or cold. Makes 3 cups.

SPICED PEACHES

½ c. water
½ c. sugar
1 T. ginger
1 clove
2 c. sliced peaches

Combine water, sugar, ginger and clove in a small saucepan. Bring to a boil and add peaches. Reduce heat and simmer until peaches are tender, about 10 minutes. Refrigerate until ready to serve.

TASTY APPLE PIE

Crust:

1½ c. all-purpose flour
½ t. salt
½ c. plus 1 T. shortening
4½ T. water

Filling:

⅔ c. sugar
1 T. flour
½ t. cinnamon
Dash cloves
1 1-lb. 4-oz. can sliced apples
1 T. milk

Crust: Sift together flour and salt; cut in shortening with pastry blender. Add water. Mix with fork until dough forms a ball. Turn out on lightly floured board. Shape into ball; cut in half. Form one half into a flat circle, roll out to fit 8-inch pie pan. Place loosely in pan.

Filling: Mix together sugar, flour, cinnamon and cloves. Add to apple; mix well. Turn into pan lined with crust. Roll out second portion of crust to a circle 10 inches in diameter. Perforate with fork. Wet edge of bottom crust. Place perforated circle on top. Fold the 1 inch of extra dough under edge of bottom crust. Crimp edge. Brush top with milk. Bake in preheated 400° oven 45 to 50 minutes. Pie may be served warm, topped with coarsely grated American cheese.

EASY RAISIN COFFEE CAKE

1½ c. sifted all-purpose flour
½ t. salt
6 T. sugar
2 t. baking powder
½ t. allspice
¾ c. milk
1 egg
3 T. butter, melted
½ c. raisins
¼ c. sugar
1 t. cinnamon

Sift together flour, salt, 6 tablespoons sugar, baking powder and allspice. Add milk, egg and butter. Mix thoroughly. Stir in raisins. Turn into greased and floured 8-inch layer cake pan. Mix together ¼ cup sugar and cinnamon. Sprinkle over top of cake. Let stand 5 minutes. Bake in preheated 350° oven 25 to 30 minutes. Cool slightly. Serve warm.

QUICK PINEAPPLE COFFEE CAKE

1½ c. sifted all-purpose flour
2 t. baking powder
¼ t. salt
2 T. sugar
1 egg
½ c. milk
⅓ c. shortening, melted
⅓ c. crushed pineapple, well drained
2 T. honey
1 T. butter, melted
3 T. chopped pecans

Sift together flour, baking powder, salt and sugar. Beat egg. Add milk and cooled shortening. Pour into flour mixture; stir only until dry ingredients are moistened. Turn into greased and floured 8-inch round layer cake pan. Mix pineapple, honey and butter together. Spoon pineapple topping over batter. Sprinkle nuts on top. Bake in preheated 400° oven 30 minutes. Serve warm.

ICE CREAM CRISPIES DESSERT

¼ c. butter
½ c. chopped walnuts or pecans
½ c. coconut
1¼ c. Rice Crispies
1 qt. vanilla ice cream

Mix butter, nuts, coconut and Rice Crispies and toast in a pan in a preheated 300° oven, for 30 minutes, stirring occasionally. Remove from oven and cool. Line an 8 x 8-inch pan with mixture, saving some for topping. Cut ice cream into slices, about 1¼ inches thick. Place over mixture in pan and sprinkle with topping. Freeze until firm.

Maysie Newsom

Quick Pineapple Coffee Cake

SOUR CREAM APPLE PIE

1 unbaked 8-inch pastry shell
2 eggs, beaten
½ c. sugar
2 T. all-purpose flour
¼ t. salt
1 T. lemon juice
1 c. dairy sour cream
4 c. thin apple slices
   Crumble Topping

Combine eggs, sugar, flour, salt and lemon juice; mix well. Stir in sour cream. Place apples in pastry shell; pour sour cream mixture over apples. Sprinkle with Crumble Topping. Bake in a preheated 400° oven 35 to 40 minutes.

CRUMBLE TOPPING

¼ c. all-purpose flour
¼ c. firmly packed brown sugar
¼ c. chopped walnuts
½ t. cinnamon
⅛ t. salt
3 T. butter

Combine flour, sugar, walnuts, cinnamon and salt; cut in butter until mixture resembles coarse crumbs.

STOVE-TOP BAKED APPLES

¼ c. sugar
   Dash cinnamon
2 large baking apples
   Butter
½ c. water

Core apples and place in a medium saucepan. Add water. Pour half of sugar into center of each apple, dab with butter, and sprinkle with cinnamon. Cook covered over medium heat; bring to a boil. Reduce heat and simmer until tender, about 20 minutes. Serve warm.

Joan C. Callahan

APPLESAUCE CAKE

½ c. shortening
1 c. sugar
1 egg
½ t. vanilla
1 t. baking soda
1 c. applesauce
½ c. chopped walnuts
1 c. golden raisins
1¾ c. sifted all-purpose flour
1 t. cinnamon
½ t. cloves
⅛ t. allspice
½ t. salt

Cream shortening; add sugar and cream again. Beat in egg and vanilla. Add baking soda to applesauce; beat until foamy. Blend into first mixture. Stir in walnuts and raisins mixed with sifted dry ingredients. Pour into greased and floured 8 x 4 x 2-inch loaf pan. Bake in preheated 325° oven 70 to 75 minutes.

COCONUT KISSES

2 egg whites
1 c. granulated sugar
1 small can coconut

Beat egg whites until they stand in peaks. Gradually add sugar; beat again until stiff. Add coconut. Drop by teaspoonful on an ungreased cookie sheet. Bake in a 250° oven 25 minutes. Do not preheat oven. Makes 2 dozen.

Mrs. P. G. Dennison

PEANUT BUTTER COOKIES

1 c. peanut butter (creamy or crunchy)
1 egg
1 c. sugar
1 t. vanilla

Mix all ingredients together, until smooth. Drop by teaspoon on cookie sheet. Flatten with a fork. Bake in a preheated 350° oven for 10 minutes. There is no flour in this recipe.

Joan C. Callahan

To measure brown sugar: Pack firmly into standard measuring cup so sugar holds shape of cup when turned out.

Chocolate Coffee Drops

CHOCOLATE COFFEE DROPS

2¼ c. all-purpose flour
1 T. baking powder
1 t. salt
2 t. ground nutmeg
2 t. ground cinnamon
2 T. boiling water
2 T. instant coffee
⅔ c. shortening
1 c. dark brown sugar, firmly packed
1 egg
1 t. vanilla
1 12-oz. pkg. chocolate chips
½ c. chopped nuts

Stir together flour, baking powder, salt, nutmeg and cinnamon. In small bowl, pour boiling water over coffee; cool. Cream shortening and sugar together until light and fluffy. Beat in egg and vanilla. Add flour alternately with coffee mixture. Stir in chocolate chips and nuts. Drop by level tablespoonfuls on greased baking sheets. Bake in preheated 375° oven 6 to 8 minutes. Makes 4½ dozen.

TOMATO SOUP CAKE

⅓ c. shortening
1 c. sugar
1 c. golden raisins
1 10½-oz. can cream of tomato soup
1¾ c. sifted all-purpose flour
1 t. baking soda
1 t. cinnamon
1 t. allspice
Dash nutmeg

Cream shortening; add sugar and cream again. Add raisins and soup all at once. Mix well. Sift together dry ingredients. Fold into first mixture. Pour in 8 x 8 x 2-inch baking pan that has been greased and floured. Bake in preheated 350° oven 30 to 35 minutes. When cold, frost with Cooked Butter Cream Icing.

COOKED BUTTER CREAM ICING

2 T. flour
½ c. milk
¼ c. butter
¼ c. shortening
½ c. sugar
1 t. vanilla

Mix flour and milk to smooth paste. Cook, stirring constantly, until mixture thickens. Chill. Cream together butter and shortening; add sugar and cream again. Add gradually to first mixture; mix well. Add vanilla. Beat 5 minutes.

> When frosting, tuck four strips of wax paper under cake to keep plate clean.

PEACH DELIGHT

2 peaches
1 t. lemon juice
3 T. sugar
½ c. whipping cream
2 t. sugar
½ t. vanilla
2 small sponge cakes, about 4 inches in diameter, cut in small pieces

Peel and slice peaches. Add lemon juice and 3 tablespoons sugar. Let stand while preparing other ingredients. Whip cream; add 2 teaspoons sugar and vanilla. Fold together cake pieces, whipped cream and peaches. Serve immediately.

INDIVIDUAL APPLE CRISP

⅔ c. pared and sliced baking apples
2 t. water
⅛ c. granulated sugar
⅛ c. brown sugar
Dash salt
⅛ t. nutmeg
⅛ t. cinnamon
½ of ⅓ c. flour
⅛ c. butter

Place half of the apples and 1 teaspoon water in each of two custard cups. Combine sugars, salt, spices and flour in a bowl; cut in butter with pastry blender. Sprinkle crumb mixture in each custard cup. Place cups on cookie sheet and bake in a preheated 375° oven about 25 minutes. Serve warm or cold. Garnish with whipped cream.

> 1 ounce chocolate equals 3 tablespoons cocoa plus 1 tablespoon fat.

TWO-WAY JELLY ROLL

3 eggs
1 c. sugar
1 c. sifted cake flour
1 t. baking powder
¼ t. salt
⅓ c. hot water
1 t. vanilla
   Confectioners' sugar
⅓ c. strawberry or raspberry jelly
½ pt. strawberry or chocolate ice cream

Beat eggs until thick and light-colored. Add sugar gradually, beating constantly. Sift together flour, baking powder and salt. At low speed, blend dry ingredients, water and vanilla into egg mixture just until combined. Turn into greased and floured 10 x 15-inch jelly roll pan. Bake in preheated 375° oven 15 to 20 minutes. Cut in half lengthwise. Turn out on clean towel, lightly dusted with confetioners' sugar. Trim edges.

Jelly Roll: Beat jelly with fork. Spread on half of warm roll. Roll up; wrap in towel. Cool on cake rack.

Ice Cream Roll: Sprinkle half of warm roll with confectioners' sugar. Roll up in towel. Place on cake rack; let stand until cold. Unroll. Place firm ice cream in bowl; mash slightly. Do not allow to melt. Spread on cake roll. Roll again; wrap in foil. Freeze until firm.

BUTTERSCOTCH CANDY DROPS

1 6-oz. pkg. butterscotch morsels
2 T. peanut butter
¼ c. rolled oats
¼ c. bran flakes
¼ c. finely chopped walnuts

Mix together all ingredients. Melt over low heat. Drop by teaspoonfuls in miniature crinkled paper cups. Chill until firm. Makes two dozen.

BROWNIES

4 eggs, beaten
1 c. sugar
1 stick butter
1 large (1 lb.) can Hershey Chocolate Syrup
¾ c. nuts
1 c. flour

Combine ingredients and mix well. Pour into lightly greased jelly roll or large cake pan. Bake in a preheated 350° oven 25 minutes.

FROSTING

1⅓ c. sugar
6 T. butter
6 T. milk
4 large marshmallows
½ c. chocolate chips

Bring sugar, butter and milk to boil slowly. Boil one minute or until soft ball stage. Remove from heat and add marshmallows and chocolate chips. Stir until partly cooled. Spread.

RELISH IDEAS

CARROT CURLS: Pare carrots. With a vegetable peeler, slice carrots lengthwise, starting at thick end. Wind each strip around finger; fasten with wooden pick. Place in ice water. When ready to serve, remove wooden picks. Carrots will remain curled.

CELERY STICKS: Cut leaves from celery. Separate celery and cut in 3 to 4 inch lengths. Slit in narrow strips at both ends almost to center. Soak in ice water until crisp and curled.

RADISH ROSES: Cut off root end. Leave on ½-inch stem. Cut through skin with a paring knife from root end down to form 4 or 5 thin petals around radish. Place in ice water to open. Arrange vegetables on large serving platter or relish tray.

CURRY CANAPÉS

- ¾ c. cheddar cheese, shredded
- ½ c. ripe olives, chopped
- ¼ c. chopped scallions
- ¼ c. mayonnaise
- ½ t. curry powder
- 1 small loaf party rye

In a small bowl mix all ingredients together. Spread on party rye cut cornerwise. Broil until bubbly. Spread will stay fresh for one month when refrigerated and kept in a covered container.

Joan C. Callahan

HAM PUFFS

- ½ t. cream of tartar
- 1 egg
- 1 c. grated American cheese
- 1 small can deviled ham (4¾ oz.)
- 2½ dozen toasted, buttered, bread rounds

Combine cream of tartar, egg and cheese; fold in ham. Spread mixture on bread rounds. Place on cookie sheet, and broil.

Joan C. Callahan

SWISS CHEESE FONDUE

- 1 8-oz. pkg. natural Swiss cheese sliced, cut into strips
- 1 T. flour
- ¼ t. dry mustard
- 1 clove garlic, cut in half
- 1 c. dry white wine
  Dash salt
  Dash white pepper
  Dash nutmeg
- 2 T. Kirsch
  French or Vienna bread

Toss together cheese with flour and mustard. Rub inside of fondue cooker, chafing dish or electric skillet with garlic. Pour in the wine, and heat until bubbles rise to the surface. (NEVER let it boil.) Add cheese mixture—½ cup at a time—and stir constantly, letting each amount melt completely before adding another. Continue stirring until mixture bubbles lightly. Stir in seasonings and Kirsch. Keep fondue bubbling while serving. Serve with bite-size chunks of bread with a crusty edge for dunking into the fondue. If fondue becomes too thick, pour in a little warmed wine.

COCKTAIL SAUSAGES

- Cocktail sausages
- ⅓ c. mustard
- ½ c. grape jelly

Cut sausages into bite-size pieces. Heat mustard and jelly in a small saucepan; add meat. Continue to heat, stirring occasionally. Simmer for 10 minutes. Serve on crackers.

Crab Meat Dip

SPINACH DIP

2 c. mayonnaise
½ c. chopped onions
½ c. chopped parsley
1 10-oz. package chopped spinach, defrosted and well drained
⅛ t. garlic salt
Dash pepper

Mix spinach, onions, parsley and seasonings together; add mayonnaise a bit at a time. Chill. Allow flavors to blend before serving.

Joan C. Callahan

CRAB MEAT DIP

4 oz. cream cheese
Dash salt
½ T. onion, grated
1 t. lemon juice
¼ t. Worcestershire sauce
6 T. sour cream
1 7-oz. can crab meat

Cheese should be at room temperature. Add remaining ingredients and mix together. Chill before serving.

NOTE: If desired, top with minced pimiento for color.

49

Assorted Vegetable Platter
  with Dill Dip, page 51
Hot Hors d'Oeuvres
Tasty Ham Triangles, page 51
Pizza Fondue with Bread Cubes, page 51

HOT HORS D'OEUVRES

Bacon slices, cut in half
Shrimp
Chicken liver
Water chestnuts
Green olives
Cream cheese

For each tidbit, wrap bacon slices around any of these ingredients, and secure with a toothpick. Olives may be cut in half and stuffed with cream cheese. In a shallow pan, broil for 7 minutes on each side.

DILL DIP

1 c. sour cream   ½ t. salt
¾ t. dill weed   ¼ t. grated onion

Combine ingredients and chill. Serve with raw vegetables, or crackers. May also be used with baked potatoes.

HOT CHEESE PUFFS

¼ c. soft butter
½ lb. grated sharp cheddar cheese
1 c. flour
1 dash cayenne pepper

Mix all ingredients well and chill for at least one hour. Roll into small balls and place on an ungreased cookie sheet, flattening slightly. Bake in preheated 400° oven for 5 minutes. Makes 4 dozen.

Sis Dennison

PIZZA FONDUE

 1 onion, chopped
½ lb. ground beef
 2 10½-oz. cans pizza sauce
   (or tomato sauce)
 1 T. cornstarch
1½ t. fennel seed
1½ t. oregano
¼ t. garlic powder
10 oz. grated cheddar cheese
 1 c. grated mozzarella cheese

Brown onion and ground beef in a large sauce pan. Mix pizza sauce and cornstarch together and add to meat. Add fennel seed, oregano and garlic powder to this mixture. Just before serving, add cheddar and mozzarella cheese. Stir over medium heat until cheeses are melted. Pour into fondue pot. Serve with garlic bread cubes or French bread cubes.

APRICOT AND BACON TWISTS

Bacon
Apricots
Walnuts

For each tidbit, wrap partially cooked bacon strip around dried apricot half and a walnut half. Secure with toothpick. Broil until bacon is crisp, about 3 minutes.

TOASTED ONION STRIPS

 1 envelope onion soup mix
 1 c. soft butter
12 slices white bread

Mix onion soup and butter together. Spread mixture on slices of bread; remove crust. Slice bread into 5 strips. Place on baking sheet and bake in a preheated 375° oven for 10 minutes or until golden brown. Makes 5 dozen strips.

Joan C. Callahan

TASTY HAM TRIANGLES

10 slices sandwich bread, toasted
¼ lb. (1 c.) ham, chopped
 2 ozs. (½ c.) shredded cheddar cheese
 4 pimiento stuffed olives, chopped
¼ c. sweet pickle relish, drained
½ c. salad dressing
   Few drops onion juice
   Paprika
   Pimiento strips
   Parsley sprigs

Trim crusts from toast. Cut in half diagonally; then in half again. Mix together ham, cheese, olives, relish, salad dressing and onion juice. Spread on toast triangles. Broil 4 to 6 minutes. Sprinkle with paprika; garnish with pimiento strips and parsley. Makes 40 triangles.

PEPPER STEAK

3 lbs. sirloin steak, 1½ inches thick
½ c. soy sauce
1 clove garlic
1 c. beef bouillon
2 green peppers, sliced
2 onions, sliced
1 t. pepper
5 stalks celery, sliced
2 T. cornstarch
   Tomato wedges

Marinate meat in mixture of soy sauce, garlic, and ½ cup beef bouillon for 15 minutes. Drain meat, reserving liquid. Melt a piece of fat trimmed from steak, in a very hot frying pan. Quickly brown meat on each side. Add onion, celery, and green pepper and cook until tender. Mix cornstarch with reserved liquid and remaining beef bouillon; stir into meat and vegetables. Cook until thickened. Serve with rice. Tomato wedges may be added for garnish. Serves 8.

CREAMED CHICKEN IN CONFETTI RICE RING

¼ c. butter or margarine
⅓ c. flour
1⅓ c. chicken broth
1⅓ c. light cream
¾ t. salt
¾ t. paprika
⅛ t. white pepper
1½ t. onion juice
2 c. cooked chicken, cubed
½ c. blanched, slivered almonds
2 T. sherry
   Confetti Rice Ring

Melt butter over low heat. Add flour; stir until bubbly. Blend in broth and cream. Cook while stirring in salt, paprika, pepper, onion juice, chicken and almonds. Heat 10 minutes. Blend in sherry just before serving. Serve in Confetti Rice Ring. Serves 8.

CONFETTI RICE RING

6 to 8 c. hot cooked white rice
¼ c. soft butter
⅔ c. finely chopped parsley
3 T. diced pimiento

Combine ingredients. Pack firmly into buttered 6-cup ring mold. Unmold at once. If not used immediately, keep warm by covering with foil and placing in pan of hot water.

BUFFET MEAT LOAF

1½ lbs. ground beef
½ lb. ground pork
3 c. soft bread crumbs
1 egg
1 medium onion, minced
¾ c. milk
2 t. salt
1¼ t. ginger
2 c. peeled chopped cooking apples
1½ c. instant mashed potatoes
1 10-oz. pkg. frozen, chopped broccoli, cooked and drained
½ c. shredded cheddar cheese

In a bowl blend together beef and pork. Add bread crumbs, egg, onion, milk, salt and ginger; lightly mix to blend. Stir in apples. On a 15 x 10-inch jelly roll pan, shape into a loaf. Bake in a preheated 350° oven 45 minutes. Drain off excess fat. Prepare mashed potatoes according to package directions. Combine potatoes and broccoli; frost loaf with potato mixture. Sprinkle top with cheddar cheese and bake 15 additional minutes. Let stand about 5 minutes before removing to a warmed platter. Serves 8 to 10.

Mock Sauerbraten

MOCK SAUERBRATEN

1 c. Italian dressing
1 c. water
6 bay leaves
10 whole cloves
4 peppercorns
⅛ t. ground ginger
4 lbs. beef rump roast
½ c. water
⅔ c. crumbled gingersnaps

In large bowl, combine Italian dressing, 1 cup water, bay leaves, cloves, peppers and ginger. Add meat, turning to coat; cover and marinate in refrigerator about 24 hours. In large saucepan or Dutch oven, brown meat; add marinade. Simmer covered, 2 hours or until tender. Strain liquid from meat into medium saucepan and combine with ½ cup water and gingersnaps; cook, stirring constantly until smooth. Serves 8.

Asparagus with Rarebit Sauce

SCALLOPED POTATOES AND HAM

8 c. potatoes, sliced	3 T. butter
4 c. ham, diced	2 T. flour
3 medium onions, sliced	Dash pepper
	2¼ c. milk
2 t. salt	

Add potatoes and onions to medium sauce-pan. Cover with water and bring to a boil; cook until tender. Melt butter in a medium saucepan. Remove from heat; add flour, pepper and salt stirring until smooth. Stir in milk. Return to heat; boil until mixture thickens. Layer mixture of potatoes, ham and onions in a greased casserole dish, topping each layer with sauce. Bake, uncovered for 35 minutes. Serves 8.

SHRIMP CREOLE

 2 lbs. shrimp
⅓ c. butter
⅔ c. onion, chopped
⅔ c. green pepper, chopped
⅔ c. sliced mushrooms
 1 c. celery
 1 clove garlic
 1 T. lemon juice
 3 T. flour
 2 8-oz. cans tomato paste
 2 8-oz. cans tomato sauce
½ t. salt
⅛ t. pepper
½ t. dried basil

Sauté onion, green pepper, mushrooms, garlic and celery in melted butter until tender. Stir in flour; bring to a boil. Add tomato sauce and paste, salt, basil, lemon juice and pepper. Cook for 10 minutes. Add shrimp, and bring to a boil. Reduce heat and simmer until thoroughly heated. Pour over rice. Serves 8.

ASPARAGUS WITH RAREBIT SAUCE

¼ c. butter
¼ c. flour
 1 t. salt
⅓ t. white pepper
⅓ t. dry mustard
 1 c. milk
1¼ c. (5 oz.) shredded cheddar cheese
 2 lbs. fresh asparagus, cooked (approximately 32 stalks)
 4 c. cooked rice
 8 slices bacon cooked crisp

Melt butter in large saucepan. Stir in flour, salt, pepper and dry mustard. Slowly add milk to flour and butter mixture. Cook over low heat stirring constantly until mixture thickens and is smooth.

Remove from heat and add cheese; stir until cheese melts. Arrange 3 to 4 stalks heated asparagus on ½ cup portion rice. Pour ¼ cup rarebit sauce over asparagus. Top with strip of bacon. Serves 8.

SHISH KEBAB PARTY

For easy entertaining, try shish kebabs. They are simple to prepare and provide a complete meal. If you wish, you may serve the ingredients on a platter and let your guests make their own favorite combinations. The following is a list of suggested foods to choose from. Place combinations on skewers and cook, turning and basting occasionally, to desired doneness. Marinades may be used to tenderize and flavor the meat.

Beef Shish Kebabs

Beef tenderloin cubes
Hamburger balls
Lamb cubes
Pork cubes
Ham cubes
Bacon slices, partially fried
Sausage links
Chicken livers
Cherry tomatoes
Fresh mushrooms
Cooked carrot slices
Green or red pepper chunks
Canned new potatoes
Pineapple chunks
Spiced apples
Banana slices

MARINADES

LAMB MARINADE

1 clove garlic
½ c. onion, chopped
½ t. oregano
½ t. thyme
½ t. pepper
1¼ t. salt
½ c. salad oil
⅓ c. lemon juice

Combine seasonings with salad oil and lemon juice. Mix thoroughly. Add lamb cubes and mix until each is well coated. Marinate overnight.

RED WINE MARINADE

2 c. red wine
1 c. tomato puree
2 T. wine vinegar
3 cloves garlic, crushed
1 T. salt
½ t. freshly ground pepper
1 t. thyme

Combine wine, tomato puree and vinegar. Mix well. Stir in all other ingredients. Pour over pieces of meat and let stand overnight.

Sis Dennison

TERIYAKI MARINADE

1 t. ginger
1 clove garlic, minced
⅓ c. onion, grated
2 T. sugar
½ c. soy sauce
¼ c. water

Combine ingredients and mix well. Pour over beef cubes and refrigerate, covered, for at least two hours.

HONEY-GARLIC MARINADE

½ c. honey
½ c. soy sauce
2 cloves garlic, crushed
3 T. catsup

Mix ingredients together; add meat chunks and marinate 12 hours or longer, turning occasionally.

Sis Dennison

SAUCES FOR DIPPING

HOT SAUCE

1 T. vinegar
1 t. lemon juice
¼ c. oil
1¼ c. chili sauce
1 t. tabasco sauce
¼ t. garlic salt
½ t. dry mustard
1 T. onion, minced

Combine ingredients. Bring to a boil; simmer for 15 minutes. Serve warm or store in refrigerator.

MUSTARD SAUCE FOR PORK

½ c. sugar
1 t. flour
½ c. bouillon
½ c. prepared mustard
½ c. vinegar
¼ c. butter
3 egg yolks

Mix dry ingredients. Add to liquids in double boiler, and cook for ½ hour.

Peggy Jacobs

BAR-B-Q SAUCE

1 c. tomato catsup
½ c. cider vinegar
1 t. sugar
1 t. chili powder
Pinch salt
1½ c. water
3 stalks celery, chopped
3 bay leaves
1 clove garlic
2 T. onion, chopped
4 T. butter
4 T. Worcestershire sauce
1 t. paprika
Dash black pepper

Combine all ingredients and bring to a boil. Simmer for 15 minutes. Remove from heat and strain.

SWEET AND SOUR SAUCE FOR MEATBALLS

2 13-oz. cans pineapple chunks
1½ c. chicken broth
¼ c. brown sugar
¾ c. vinegar
1 T. soy sauce
1 T. catsup
4 T. cornstarch
1 c. green onions, thinly sliced
3 green peppers, cut in chunks

Drain pineapple chunks and set aside, retaining liquid. Combine liquid with remaining ingredients except onions and peppers; cook until thick. Add green onions and peppers; cook 1 minute longer. Remove from heat and add pineapple chunks. Serve immediately or refrigerate.

Peggy Jacobs

FRUIT COMPOTE

1 large can pears
1 large can peaches
1 large can pineapple
1 large can Bing cherries
　Brandy to taste
1½ T. slivered orange peel

Drain juices from the canned fruit. Add orange peel to the juice and simmer in a large saucepan for 30 minutes. Add fruit and continue to heat. Stir in brandy. Serve hot poured over ice cream.

APPLE CARAMEL

10 apples	½ c. butter
⅔ c. sugar	1 t. vanilla

Pare and core apples; cut into 8 pieces. Melt sugar over a low flame, in a large heavy skillet; stir constantly until sugar is melted and golden brown. Add butter and blend. Add apples to mixture; stir. Simmer covered for 10 minutes, or until apples are cooked. Add vanilla and stir. Serve warm with cream.

Joan C. Callahan

CHERRY BERRY JUBILEE

⅓ c. currant jelly
2 T. cornstarch
1 1-lb. pkg. frozen whole strawberries, thawed
1 1-lb. can dark, sweet, pitted cherries in heavy syrup, drained
¼ c. brandy
1 qt. vanilla ice cream

Mix jelly and cornstarch in saucepan. Drain strawberries; reserve ¾ cup syrup and add to jelly mixture. Place over low heat; stir and cook mixture until thickened. Add drained fruit and heat thoroughly; pour into chafing dish; add brandy and hold lighted match near it. Spoon flaming sauce over individual servings of ice cream. Serves 8.

RHUBARB CRISP

4 c. rhubarb, sliced
½ c. butter
¾ c. brown sugar, firmly packed
½ c. all-purpose flour
½ t. cinnamon
1 c. oatmeal

Arrange rhubarb in shallow baking dish. Cream butter; blend in sugar, flour, and cinnamon. Stir in oatmeal. Sprinkle mixture over rhubarb. Bake in preheated 375° oven 25 to 30 minutes. Serve warm.

NOTE: Lemon juice may be sprinkled over rhubarb for added tartness.

Joan C. Callahan

BLUEBERRY BUCKLE

½ c. butter
1 c. sugar
2 eggs
2 t. vanilla
2 c. all-purpose flour
2 t. baking powder
½ t. salt
⅔ c. milk
4 c. blueberries

Cream butter and sugar together. Beat in egg and vanilla. Sift together dry ingredients. Stir into sugar mixture, alternating with milk. Pour into a greased 13 x 9-inch baking dish. Add blueberries to cover cake batter.

TOPPING

1 c. sugar	1 t. cinnamon
⅔ c. all-purpose flour	Dash nutmeg
	½ c. butter

Combine dry ingredients. Cut butter into flour mixture until crumbly. Sprinkle over blueberries. Bake in a preheated 375° oven 40 to 45 minutes. Allow to cool slightly before serving.

PEACH DESSERT

3 egg whites
1 c. granulated sugar
17 soda crackers
¼ c. coarse walnuts
1 t. vanilla
1 large can peaches (sliced)
½ pt. whipping cream

Beat egg whites until stiff. Gradually add sugar and beat again until very stiff. Crumble soda crackers by hand, not too fine. Add crumbled crackers, walnuts, and vanilla to egg and sugar mixture. Spread mixture into a greased 13 x 9 x 2-inch pan, and bake in a preheated 350°oven 25-30 minutes. Let cool. Thoroughly drain peach slices and pat dry. Fold into stiffly whipped cream and spread on crust. Refrigerate overnight. Serves 8-10.

Mrs. P. G. Dennison

TWINKIE TORTE

8 Twinkies
1 12-oz. package semisweet chocolate chips
2 T. water
2 T. sugar
3 eggs, separated
2½ pts. whipped cream
¾ c. chopped toasted almonds or pecans

Split Twinkies in half and arrange in a 13- x 9-inch pan. Melt chocolate chips with water and sugar; cool. Add egg yolks to chocolate, stirring well. Beat egg whites until stiff and fold into chocolate mixture. Whip ½ pint whipped cream and add to chocolate mixture. Pour chocolate over Twinkies. Refrigerate for several hours or overnight. Before serving, top with remaining whipped cream. Sprinkle with chopped almonds or pecans.

Joan C. Callahan

EASY PECAN PIE

3 eggs
½ c. sugar
4 T. melted butter
¼ t. salt
1 c. dark corn syrup
1 t. vanilla
1 c. pecans
1 uncooked pie shell

Break eggs into a bowl, but do not beat. Add other ingredients and mix well. Pour into uncooked pie shell, and bake in a preheated 350° oven 30 minutes or until mixture is set.

BRANDY PECAN PUDDING

4 large eggs
1 c. sugar
1⅓ c. light corn syrup
⅓ c. butter
3 T. brandy
1½ t. vanilla
1 c. chopped pecans
Vanilla ice cream

Beat eggs, sugar, syrup, butter, brandy, and vanilla together in a large bowl until thoroughly mixed. Add pecans and stir. Pour into a buttered square baking pan. Bake for 40 minutes in a 375° oven. Cool slightly. Serve warm, with ice cream.

Joan C. Callahan

VENETIAN TORTE

1 3-oz. pkg. lime-flavored gelatin
1 3-oz. pkg. raspberry-flavored gelatin
3 c. boiling water
3 c. miniature marshmallows
1 13½-oz. can drained, crushed pineapple
1 c. whipping cream
12 lady fingers, cut in half lengthwise

Dissolve each package of gelatin separately in 1½ cups water; pour into 8-inch square pans. Chill until firm; cut in cubes. Combine marshmallows, pineapple and gelatin cubes; mix lightly. Whip cream. Fold in whipped cream; pour into a 9-inch springform pan lined with ladyfingers. Chill several hours. Serves 8 to 10.

BAKED PEACHES

5 to 6 large peaches
1 can fruit cocktail, drained
¾ c. chopped walnuts
Brandy to taste
Whipped cream

Peel peaches; cut in half and remove stones. Place in a shallow baking dish. Fill each cavity with mixture of fruit cocktail and nuts. Bake in preheated 350° oven for 20 minutes. Pour brandy over peaches and chill until ready to serve. Top with whipped cream.

NOTE: Whipped cream may be prepared ahead of time and kept chilled in the refrigerator, along with peaches, until ready to serve.

Whipping cream when whipped, doubles in volume.

EASY FRUITCAKE

2 c. flour
1½ c. sugar
2 t. baking soda
½ t. salt
1 1-lb. can fruit cocktail
2 eggs
½ c. walnuts or pecans
½ c. brown sugar

Sift flour, sugar, soda and salt together. Add fruit, juice, eggs, and nuts. Beat for 3 minutes; pour into greased 13 x 9-inch cake pan. Sprinkle brown sugar on top. Bake in a preheated 325° oven for 50 minutes.

BUTTER SAUCE

1 c. butter
¾ c. sugar
⅔ c. evaporated milk
½ t. vanilla

Boil first 3 ingredients over medium heat for 7 minutes. Add vanilla. Serve hot over cake.

INDEX

NOTES

A very special thank you to the following for their cooperation and use of their recipes and photos: American Dairy Association of Wisconsin, California Apricot Advisory Board, National Livestock and Meat Board, Reynolds Metal Company, Self-Rising Flour and Cornmeal Program Incorporated, Wisconsin Gas Company.

Cover Recipes: Tossed Green Salad, page 8
Green Peas With Pearl Onions, page 14
Wild Rice, page 17
Cornish Game Hens, page 30